Unsafe Monuments

Jennifer Copley

ARROWHEAD
PRESS

First published 2006 by
Arrowhead Press
70 Clifton Road, Darlington
Co. Durham, DL1 5DX
Tel: (01325) 260741

Typeset in 11pt Laurentian by
Arrowhead Press

Email: editor@arrowheadpress.co.uk
Website: http://www.arrowheadpress.co.uk

© *Jennifer Copley 2006*

ISBN-10: 1-904852-13-0
ISBN-13: 978-1-904852-13-1

All rights reserved. No part of this book may be reproduced, stored in a retrieval system, or transmitted in any form, or by any means, electronic, mechanical, photocopying, recording or otherwise, without prior written permission from the author or Arrowhead Press.

Requests to publish works from this book should be sent to Arrowhead Press.

Jennifer Copley has asserted her right under Section 77 of the Copyright, Designs and Patents Act 1988 to be identified as the author of this work.

Arrowhead Press is a member of
Independent Northern Publishers.

Printed by Athenaeum Press, Gateshead, Tyne and Wear.

ERRATUM
Page 38

3

In the gardens, flowers have gangrene.
No one knows how this has happened.
They say to each other,
We have watered and fed them
all their lives. Now we have nothing
to take to the cemetery.

for Martin

with special thanks to Richard and Gareth

Acknowledgements

Thanks are due to the editors of the following publications in which some of the poems in this book have appeared:

Acumen
Equinox
Obsessed with Pipework
Other Poetry
Rain Dog
Seam
Smiths Knoll
The Interpreter's House
The Long Islander
The North

Blinking Eye Anthology 2004
Lancaster Lit. Fest. Anthology 2005
Cinnamon Press Anthology 2006.

House won 1st prize in the *Ottakar's & Faber National Poetry Competition 2006*

Ice in August was shortlisted for the *Strokestown Prize* in 2005.

Small Island and *Minding the Angels* were privately commissioned by Dr. Martin Angel in 2005

Contents

Unsafe Monument	7
The Lost House	8
Pomegranates	11
The Sorrow Dress	12
Blue Net Gloves	13
Aunt Alexina	14
Gardening with Hymns	15
House	16
Miss Wilkinson	17
Camels	18
The Gluttons	19
Bride to Be	20
Mary Ann	21
Old Elsa	22
Wolves	23
The Fugitive	24
The Island	25
Scrapbook	26
S and D	27
The Poacher	28
Greed	29
Jake	30
Wastwater	31
Ice in August	32
Walking on Water	33
Sea Love	34
Washing the Dead	35
Small Island	36
The Village	37
Adulterous Women	40
Indian Bracelets	41
Up to his Ears	42
The Tree-Eater	43
The Orchard	44

Apples	45
The Tree	46
Painters	47
If I Turned up One Sunday	48
Fish and the Bank-Manager	49
The Accountant	50
There	51
Razor	52
Monday	53
Funeral Plans	54
Bedroom	55
The Tear	56
Weather	57
Writing a Love Poem	58
Ten Places Where I See My Mother	59
Speaking with the Dead	60
Angels in the North	61
Wallflowers	62
Minding the Angels	63

Unsafe Monument

The angel's mouth is a silent O
although his lips appear pink
as dawn rises. He has no teeth
but a spider's web crosses and re-crosses
lip to lip.

He carries a lyre through which the wind
plays tunes. When he was young and gleaming,
pristine from the factory,
he could accompany himself.
Now his throat is in holes.

Eliza, aged 3 days,
safe in the arms of Jesus.
The angel with bent head
reads once again
the upside-down words.

His hair still curls
as if his mother comes each night
and rolls it round her finger.
She can't repair his wings.
They lie in the grass
with cellophane scraps and flower-heads.

The Lost House

1

When I came home, there was no house
only a hole and shrivelled garden grass.
The path was still there, gravel ending in a neat line
expecting the red front door we'd painted in fits and starts
last summer.

I looked all round. In the ditch was a tap
and a torn curtain. In the far corner, two chair legs.
Wedged under the hedge, Matthew's toy horse,
intact, the stirrups swinging
as if he'd just got off.

I looked up. There was the chimney
perched on a cloud like a hat.
All day I searched –
my children, my husband, my cat –
calling under trees, spreading out a map inked with their names.
I followed a stream for miles to find one ballet shoe.

Yesterday the smell of the hall
slid under my nose for a minute.
Today I kept seeing my wellingtons
walking round the edges of my eyes.
I knew they were mine; my daughter's have an S
for Sarah, biroed just inside the top.

I've had to buy a new wardrobe.
I carry it on my back, ceaselessly searching
for our bedroom to put it in.
I thought I saw my fridge the other day,
in the dump, but when I got closer
the fridge magnets weren't mine.

I've got very thin with all this trailing.
People look at me strangely
when I show them a list of all I've lost,
photos of my children.
When I woke this morning, I had no tongue,
no teeth, my hair only grew
at the back of my head.

I'm getting old, forgetful
but I can still remember the smell
of my husband's skin,
how we slept like spoons;
or back to back,
our children in our arms,
their downy scalps against our lips.

2

Did I mention my cat?
I've lost him.
Is he with the others
or on his own,
desperately crying?
If you see him, he's black,
eyes like lamps, amber,
fur that smells of grass
or my bed.
Pick him up for me.
Tell him I'm looking.
I've climbed all the local trees,
spilt milk in puddles all round,
chunks of Cod Supreme With Jelly.
I don't know what else to do.

I've called and called.
If you see him, please let him in.
He won't scratch the furniture.
A rub behind the ears
and he'll go to sleep
no trouble at all.

3

I'd carried her for months,
knees and elbows sharp as the points of a star,
turning somersaults under my ribs.
I'm sure she was still there
the day I lost the others.
Looking back, it's a bit of a blank
but one day I woke exhausted from the search
and my stomach was flat as a pancake.
There was blood on the sheet.
It dripped down my thighs all day.
I spread it on bread,
used it for jam.

Pomegranates

In her room next to the closed door,
Katie lies alone between cold sheets.
She will lie there all day,
let her breasts' unwanted milk
sour the pillow. Last night
she dreamt of a man in a painting,
saved from starvation by a girl's full breast.
Milk trickled down his chin into his beard.

This year she will not buy pomegranates,
lug them home through slushy streets,
find a pin and prick out the seeds,
burst them in her mouth
like drops of blood.

Her husband will not dress the tree
with baubles, stars,
the angel with the velvet skirt.
They will not visit her sister's.
Her nephews will not ask where the baby is,
stare at the wet patches on her jumper.
The bubble-wrapped toys
will stay in the cupboard.

The Sorrow Dress

In the photo, I look like my grandmother
though I'm only four years old.
Why doesn't someone smooth the crease
from my forehead?

My mother is nursing my brother.
I'm at her knee, resting gingerly against it
as if I'm expecting the lash of her tongue
but she's smiling for the camera,
hand on my shoulder.

There's a saying: *Don't let your sorrow
come higher than your knees.*
Mine has risen like the tide
from the hem of my dress
to the sash, the smocking, the Peter Pan collar.

Blue Net Gloves
after a painting by Marc Chagall

The girl wearing blue net gloves
kisses the boy's cheek
under a blue moon.
Then she holds his sickle hand,
strokes each finger, wrist, palm.

His skin is white as paper
ruled with blue lines.
He stoops as he walks
as if through water,
weeds round his ankles.
She prays for him,
a plastic Jesus to her lips.

At meals he clamps his teeth
tightly together.
She slices a pear for him,
tries to slide it in.
She feels like a parent –
coax, threaten, coax, threaten.

She sleeps in a chair to avoid bruises
till the night she mutinies –
jumps down the stairwell,
nightdress ballooning out
so she lands lightly,
runs down the street
scarcely touching the ground.

Aunt Alexina

That day she wore her best black skirt
with her red petticoat showing a good inch
and patent leather boots.
She'd put on lipstick, kohled her eyes.

When she was gone, I followed.
It was easy at first, she went slowly as if she was cold
but among the clouds she loosened her blouse,
unpicked her plait with one hand.

I kept looking down but she pushed up
impatiently. Her skirt was holding her back
so she stepped out of it. She kicked off her boots
and they dropped like stones.

I fixed my eyes on the red petticoat.
We went through rain
and the drops stuck to her streaming hair,
changing from red to violet as we climbed a rainbow.

She trod air to let me catch up.
Moonlight shone through her,
I could see her bones.
She didn't speak,

handed me a creased brown photograph
of my lost uncle.
He had one arm round my shoulders,
the other held a baby with frail curls.

Gardening with Hymns

Grandma lives in the shed,
squeezes past as I open the door,
struggle with the Atco.

I start it up on the third pull,
Grandma perches on the grass-box,
clears her throat then counts me in:
To Be A Pilgrim, rounding the vegetable-patch,
Bread Of Heaven, skimming the borders,
My Chains Fell Off, pounding the home-stretch.

Weeding brings forth softer offerings:
Lamb Of God or *Love Divine*.
For digging, we choose
Thine Be The Glory;
Grandma's tempo perfect
for thrusting in the spade.

Sometimes she sleeps,
curled like a hedgehog amongst sacks
and seed catalogues. The door is locked
but I've seen her slip through a crack
to prune the lilac, murder slugs with salt.
She can step on snails without a shudder.

House

The back of the house doesn't see you
walk up the path, nor does my father
who has waited by the dustbins nightly for weeks
to catch us together.

When he thought we were kissing
he would bang on them,
tell me to come in straight away,
the house needed to be locked.

The house wasn't worried.
It liked the feel of us
crushed between ivy and porch,
making a nest in your duffel coat.

The windows approved of us,
our wobbling reflections,
the way we moved together
letting moonlight touch both our faces at once.

Now the door welcomes you with a big red smile.
The step has warmed itself specially.
We sit there in the sun,
spooning frothy coffee into each other's mouths

while my father and briefcase are at work.
The house winks as my mother pulls down a blind
then lets it up again. A bird flies off the roof
and settles on my hair.

Miss Wilkinson

The girls curtsied and the boys bowed.
Good Morning, Miss Wilkinson we sing-songed.

The day began with Tables, chanted in a trance,
crumbs of sleep still in our eyes,
then it was Reading from Primers.
Little Dog Turpie's severed limbs
made me sick with pity,
Rapunzel, with her thick long yellow plait,
just made me cross. She had no gumption.

Afternoons were Dancing, Scripture or Handwork.
We knew Jesus loved us, wanted us for sunbeams
as we knitted our kettle-holders.
Miss Wilkinson played the piano without looking
as we skipped In And Out The Dusky Bluebells.

Bang on three, our chairs went up on our desks
then we stood in twos for Dismissal Prayers.
Hands together, eyes closed gently,
said Miss Wilkinson.

At night before I slept,
I'd imagine Miss Wilkinson
tucked up in her secret bedroom,
somewhere in the depths of the school.

Camels

The night before their wedding,
bombs brought a ceiling down.
The cake was under the bed
but the grandfather clock somersaulted
down two flights of stairs.
Mum was sweeping up slivers
of sun and stars,
still in her nightdress,
as the groom drew up at church,
spotless, with white gloves.

A week later he had to go back,
my Dad who never held me
till I was three years old.
I hid under the table,
wondered why a strange man was kissing Mum,
joking he smelt of camels
and would she scrub the desert off his back?
As he tipped out his grip, it rained sand.

The Gluttons

When you came to my door, bedraggled,
lacquered with rain,
holding a bunch of white carnations,

breaking one off and placing it in my hair,
you smelt delicious.
I had to let you back in.

Now we are proud of ourselves.
We have eaten a whole chicken in bed,
pulled the wishbone, sworn to do better.

Things will be great from now on, we say,
we'll trust each other, be kind to each other,
then we drink champagne from each other's mouths.

Asparagus dripping with butter,
chocolates from Fortnum's,
more and more champagne.

Our smiles, our lips, our kisses,
the capabilities of our stomachs,
amaze us.

Bride To Be

She prays to him every night,
kneeling on her faded bedroom carpet.
He is young and beautiful,
with a countenance like the shining sun
in all its strength.
She has stitched the pages of Revelation
to her clothes.

When he comes, eyes flaming,
feet like burnished brass,
he will transform her house,
give her walls of jasper, doors of pearl,
gardens of yielding fruit trees.
They will never be hungry.
Her sins will disappear,
washed from her skin by saints.

She will forgive her neighbours
for their insinuations,
the doctor for poisoning her with pills,
her mother for harping on.
She will be delivered from evil,
her body will be full of light.

She will cloak it in a robe with no seam,
she will bury her dead,
she will push her face into a thornbush,
feel what it was like for him.

Mary Ann

Mary Ann will be after you, they said
when I was naughty. Who she was
they wouldn't say but she lived in the cellar
with the coal.

Dad said she didn't exist
but last night she climbed into bed with me.
I woke to threads of soot on the pillow,
cobwebs on my nightie.

She'd been playing with my dolls.
They were all wearing each other's clothes
covered with dirty fingermarks,
their hair in rat's tails.

Old Elsa

What she said was never understood –
scoured for scattered,
hoard for hard,
lattice for latch
(her door was never locked.)

She wore her wild hair
blanketed about her,
sat in summer sun, eyes closed,
by the old brick wall.
She always wore a pair of soldier's boots.

Children dared each other to creep close,
look through the rip in her petticoat
(some said her legs were hairy as a wolf's)
or read the tattooed number on her arm
(was it a spell?)

I don't know if she heard them,
what she felt,
her black eyebrows moving up and down
as she sang softly to herself, all weathers,
in her mother tongue.

Wolves

From behind my curtains, I'd watch you
going to school, pony-tail swinging,
sweet little legs in ankle-socks.
It took me a while to make it with your mum.

So far I'm a bit of a novelty so you
let me brush your toffee-coloured hair
and tell you stories.
I love the way your eyes go dark and still.

Today I climb the path,
follow it to the swings where
Pam pushes you, sings happy birthday,
rockabye baby all mixed up.

You laugh. Buttercups on your dress melt.
Here comes the wicked stepfather, Pam jokes
but later she tells me to drop the fairytales.
You're having nightmares

that Red Riding Hood and Grandmother
get mashed up together in a hairy stomach;
you're totally spooked about chimneys
and cooking pots;

and you won't go near your Wendy House –
there's a wolf inside,
eating chalk to soften his voice,
dipping his claws in flour.

The Fugitive

In fear I trail the roads,
sleep in ditches, under hedgerows.
If men find me, they throw stones,
hurl insults, set on their dogs.
They are afraid of my mark.
It squats on my forehead like a toad.

Today fog dropped like a curtain,
my feet disappeared as I walked.
I could feel my brother's ghost behind me,
taking big steps to keep up
like he did as a child.
He'd leap on my back, giggling.

Then I found the sea,
the first time I had seen waves,
heard them sucking over stones as if alive.
They licked my footprints.
A girl, collecting crabs, screamed and fled
as I loomed out of the fog.

Birds do not fly from me.
They feed on rotting remnants as I do.
I would go hungry
but my mark demands to be fed.
Picking it off like a scab is useless.
If I lost it, God would give me something worse.

The Island

When I came here last, I was young.
Uncle Jack brought me in his boat.
He rowed for a while, then I rowed.
The water was helpful,
the oars moved easily through it.

When we got here, the shore was covered
with small shells, many broken.
We broke more with our feet
crunching around.
Uncle Jack took off his shoes.

The sun went down in a skirt of red
as we sat on a bench. I wanted to skim stones
but Uncle Jack said *sit a bit*.
Up close, he stroked my back,
said I was a good girl,

slipped his fingers under my shirt.
The blue of the lake turned grey as my socks.
He took off his coat.
It said Pure New Wool on the breast pocket
where he slid his glasses.

Scrapbook

She didn't know they were lies
when she stuck them in.
Some have wrinkled at the edges,
some have worn away.

There are bus tickets smelling of his pocket,
programmes, menus, a curl from his head,
photographs (black and white)
of him squinting into the sun in Marrakesh.

When she touches them they are warm.
Nevertheless she lights a match,
puts it to the cover,
waits for it to catch;

dead things climbing
out of the river of flame
to blacken her hands.

S and D

His knock
takes her to bed
with her shoes on, makes her
go on top, black hair full-drenching
his face.

Released,
she waits for him
to leave, gets the fat black
-handled scissors, cuts his shape from
the sheet.

Next time,
she swears, she'll hack
off all his hair. There'll be
hell to pay but he'll have no more
strength left.

The Poacher

Too cold to sleep, she hears him mount the stairs,
bringing the whiff of rabbits,
blood, the traps.

As he opens the door, fields rush in
with a crackle of ice.
Owls' cries somersault over skeleton hedges.

In the damp bed, her muscles have knotted,
she can't feel her fingers,
but he unsnags her frozen hair

from the buttons of her nightdress,
kisses her goosebumps,
warms her rigid limbs.

Come morning, he's gone.
Snow covers the yard.
Icicles thick as his wrist, hang from the pump.

His footprints are inside and outside
as she guts the rabbits, hands tingling
having lain on his stomach all night.

Greed

I hide in a drawer full of dust
and other leavings.
I hear you thud about the room,
looking, looking.

You tell me things.
Why do you tell me such things?
That you are a sword
up to the hilt in love with me;
that you are a hedgehog
rolling on the fallen fruit of me.

I hide in the drawer,
six inches from your belly.
I am not pulp.
I will not be pulp
and you are not a sword
or a hedgehog.

Jake

You never brush your hair at the back,
complained my daughter,
so now I try really hard to remember.

Some things you don't want to remember
but they hog your mind: his face
that day in the street, the skin stretched
to splitting point.

A week later, he tied a rope
to the ham-hook on the pantry ceiling,
made a noose.

Collecting Amy from school was his job.
He wouldn't think of her anxious face
peering through railings,
as he selected a chair.

Wastwater

Why don't we bring him here? she says,
crouching down by the waves.
Small and frail, they come up close,
sniff her skin before they shrink away.

We look for stones to skim
but there are no flat ones
and she wants them to be perfect.
She misses you.

When she was little, I told her
about the two giants who came every night
to check she'd put her toys away.
One night she hid behind the cupboard to watch.

Now I never lie to her.
I put my hands under her armpits,
pull her up.
We wobble together on the pebbles.

Ice in August

No one in her village
can believe such heat.
She wears her coolest dress
but it still glues itself
across her shoulder-blades.
People faint in the streets,
are carried home
to drink the water dry.

As she scrubs and sweeps
she dreams of ice:
in her hair, in her ears,
on the back of her neck.
Last night she sat up late,
sewing her dress.
Pins slipped from her fingers.
The thread was damp with sweat,
no need to lick.

He badgers but she won't agree
until the weather changes,
until there is ice:
ice on the rims of carriage wheels,
ice in the lily bouquet,
ice on his knuckles
as he hands her down,
ice in needle-thin stitches
hanging from the church porch.

Walking on Water
after a paper imprint by Judy Evans

The sun goes down
wearing a black veil.
There is snow on the beach
mixed with foam so cold
we feel it through wellingtons.

Facing out to sea, cheeks numb,
lips stung with salty kisses,
we hold hands in my coat pocket,
remember that time the sea froze.

We couldn't believe we walked on water.
Under our feet, trapped fish
with needle fins,
eyeballed us through ice.

Sea Love

We undress in the sea,
zips, buttons, buckles,
the whole boiling.
Everything floats away,
my dress a red silk island
blurred by foam, your shirt
with young white arms.

You slide your hands under my armpits
and I hang like a painting,
so still, so balanced.
Your hair glistens in black curls,
drops of salt slide down
red curves of your cheeks.
I open my mouth to taste you,
clean and cold.

Washing the Dead

The dead love water.
It rinses away dirty stairways of blood,
washes through empty veins to silence echoes.

It pacifies the tips of fingers,
shoulders, elbows, dry caked lips.
It flounces over hair till it is clean.

Bruises, wounds, marks of struggle
are soothed by rivulets. Soft pools
collect on bellies that no longer breathe.

Water goes where it wants: the pocket of a palm,
the hollow of a throat. It presses on eyelids
and eyeballs, erases dreams.

Small Island

In the beginning there were two things only –
darkness and water.
On the third day, God gathered the waters
into one place and called them Seas
then he let dry land appear.

From your father's house, looking towards the point
you see a small island which you think at first
is a trick of the light.
Only when there's a lull in the waves
do you believe it.

You imagine the silence there,
slime on the rocks,
how you would be stranded,
the innocence of the tide,
how it would never take the blame;

your wet skirt drying against your knees,
your fingers the fingers of ghosts,
snagged hair,
feet white with salt
as if you had walked on water.

The Village

1

It's a place where girls can only play with girls –
Hopscotch, Skipping, Dolls.
They don't play Weddings.

Mothers sit at home crumpled
as if someone has popped their skins.
All the men are drunk.

There are spaces at table,
gaps on the sofa.
If anyone hears the sound of boots, they scream.

2

In sure and certain hope, says the priest,
no longer believing it.

At six in the morning,
tears are breaking the windows.
Parents are drowning between cold sheets.

Daughters put on odd socks,
plait their own hair,
prepare unsuitable lunch-boxes.
Later, one writes in her journal,
I am forgetting my brother's eyes.

3

In the gardens, flowers have gangrene.
No one knows how this has happened.
They say to each other,
We have watered and fed them
all their lives. Now we have nothing
to take to the cemetery.

4

A grandfather swallows laburnum seeds
until his tongue is yellow.

5

Houses are labyrinths.
People get lost between the front door
and the hall.
They can't find the stairs.
They want to lie across the beds of their sons.

6

Cupboards are full.
Grandmothers keep piling food in
but taking nothing out.
One cooks soil,
measures it into a pan,
sets the table
then they will come back.

Adulterous Women

In rural areas, her tutor says,
they bury them up to their necks
then stone their heads.

All day she thinks of it –
the men with glinting eyes
closing in on one small skull,
cracking it like a nut,
exposing brains.

Would the relatives dare
to creep back later,
weep over what was left
and pull it out?

At night she dreams –
her own mother's head caved in,
and her, the foetus,
buried eternally
in sand.

Indian Bracelets

Deep in his head he hears a woman
singing an evening raga.
Her breath is heavy with spices
when he kisses her lower lip.

In his threadbare Parker Knoll,
he dreams of army pals,
his batman, his dog,
the ponies he rode in Bangalore,
a one-eyed camel that carried him to his troop-ship.

And prostitutes, Rahel and Rani,
who would do anything
for the smallest coin in his pocket.
They loved his English moustache,
the knife creases in his khaki shorts.

He wakes from the sound of bracelets
sliding up and down thin arms.

Up to his Ears

My father is buried up to his ears in earth,
you can see his forehead, a few strands of white hair
and his blue eyes.

His friends and peers go into the deadly trees
and consider death, how it will happen to them.
This is too late for my father.

Death has already caught up with him,
giving him no time to decide.
He makes a last effort,

pushes his hands with their gangly wrists,
out of mud and leaves. His ancient wrist-watch
slides about loosely.

How can I help my father in his struggle?
The cuffs of his shirt grow colder by the minute,
his voice is muffled under soil.

Can he still breathe in the lives of other people,
the wind, the bark of dogs, the footsteps
of a man brushing up litter,

who, when he gets to my father's
hands and head, skirts round them neatly,
pausing only to remove a sweet wrapper

from my father's left ear.

The Tree-Eater

She began by eating the tips of leaves,
followed by buds which were sticky
and rasped her throat.
The twigs were a bit of a mouthful
but she managed eventually.
After a lull – drank cough syrup,
went to the toilet – she ate her first branch
and really got the taste for it.
Her skin began to prickle.
Bits of wood that wouldn't go down,
poked through like a pin-cushion.
Green-lipped, she tackled the trunk,
its boles and crevices, the odd nest,
but people were drifting away.
They'd seen something more interesting
the other side of the field.

The Orchard

She eats apples to bring him back:
his cheeks, his chest, his navel,
his pubic hair's sweet saltiness.
Each bite brings him closer.
Juice trickles down her fingers to her palm
which he will soon kiss.

She cups another in warm hands,
inhales the scent.
The skin is taut and rosy.
He will wander his lips
down the notches of her spine.

At night, breathless from her mother's slaps
for the reputation she is getting –
strange behaviour in and out of trees,
sitting in the forks of them for hours –
she grows an orchard in her head.

He'll come through the gate
in his soldier's coat, wait
in long grass littered with windfalls.
He'll roll two cigarettes.
She knows how to lick the Rizla Paper,
shelter a match in apple-scented hands.

Apples

When they start to fall,
she gathers them in her apron,
tumbles them into the basket
where they sprawl like water.

She carries them to the house,
weeds out the rotten,
the ones plugged with drugged wasps
or studded with fly.

She slices the rosiest for her sister
who is not allowed to touch the knife,
puts some in sugared water to stew.
Clouds of sweet steam fill the air,

bring her father in from the yard,
muck still on his boots.
At night she dreams of apples
and the one Adam hides

behind his back,
will not let her taste,
teasing with tales of serpents
and an angel's sword.

The Tree

As a child, she'd feared it,
run with pounding feet
from its shadow tossed across the lawn,
the limbs of its branches,
the green fringe from behind which
it watched.

As she grew, it became kinder,
softer-shaped,
its scent no longer frightened her away.
She met her first lover under it,
lost her virginity on a tablecloth
spread over moss.

She still picnics in its shade,
leans her back against a trunk
as wrinkled as her skin,
lets leaves lodge in her unkempt hair.
How beautiful is the kiss of its roots
to her feet, soothing calluses and corns.

Painters

They have been in and out all day,
treading in grit and flecks of Old Maroon.
Bill has been helping: *you've missed a bit/
that window sticks*, kind of help.
She has made countless cups of sugared tea,
emptied the biscuit barrel.

Now the long legs of ladders
are stacked on the lawn,
dust-sheets splattered with red
tucked round them.
While Bill tidies, she carries a chair outside
to admire the new skin of the house.

Don't look at me, she says
as they get undressed that night
but because the curtains are down,
nothing can stop the moonlight
diving in, swamping the pillow,
their two grey heads.

If I Turned Up One Sunday

If I turned up one Sunday
and you were wearing your dark suit
ready for church,
I could almost believe she was in the garage,
knocking mud off your best shoes.

If the kitchen smelled of burnt toast
and there were crusts in the sink,
it was like she'd left the washing up
for later, run upstairs
to comb her hair.

If there was butter softening
on the corner of the Aga,
it was as if she was thinking
of making a crumble,
just popped out to see
if there were any windfalls.

Fish and the Bank Manager

Dad's home for lunch on Saturdays,
the day the fish-man comes.
Mum waits till she hears his bell,
runs down the path in her slippers
to buy fresh plaice.

Dripping with ice, they're slapped down
on a board spread with breadcrumbs
grated from a stale loaf
then fried in the old black pan.
Dad likes the skin left on
so we all have to eat it.

He glares at us if we fidget
or don't use a napkin.
Mum gets into trouble if we misbehave
so we dab our mouths,
try not to scrape our cutlery.
We're no good at sums
but our manners are faultless

till my brother finds a bone and gags.
His glasses mist up.
He can't see what's on his fork.
Don't make a fuss, begs Mum.
Look at Dad crunching up his bones.

The Accountant

He tests them on their Tables every night.

They dread Mondays,
bringing their slice of squared paper home,
numbered 1 to 10,
wait while he counts the X's,

checks their palms, wrists,
cuffs of their shirts.
Here's where it all should be, he says,
tapping his head. *No need for fingers either.*

They get plenty of fish and carrots for brain-food
but neither show an aptitude for Maths.
Jen writes with imagination and feeling, says Miss West.
Hal's a first-class runner.

Cuts no ice with their Dad.

There

My father shows me a rip
in the seat of his pants,
pulls them off in front of the window
as the bus grinds slowly past.

We look for clean.
The bedroom's dusty but the same.
There is the photo of my mother
the last time I saw her,
the chair with her checked skirt
neatly laid across it.

On the bed is the mobile phone
we gave her after the stroke.
Dad says it doesn't work too well,
look how bristly his chin is.
Over the pillow is Mum's cardigan.
I press it to my face
but it smells of him.

Razor

You can't remember what it's for
so I take it from you,
hide it,
shave you with your old electric one.

Later I wrap you up,
put you in the car,
run you to Ennerdale
where the lake makes you cry.

There's a dedication on a bench –
Peter, your light still shines.
You ask me over and over
what it means.

We saw a hare here once.
Amazingly, you recall it,
how it loped along the road ahead of us
then dived with flattened ears
under the furze.

Monday

I sit by my father's side and comb his hair.
Because it is Monday, the nurse has bathed
and shaved him, cut his toenails
softened in soapy water.
He is obedient till she produces
pumice for his heels.
Then he sulks.

After lunch comes Linda the cleaner
so I take Dad out from under her feet.
When we get to the lake
there are no free benches
so we sit on the grass.
I undo the top button of his coat,
offer him a Polo.

He watches the water grey as ash.
I watch him, his thin shoulders,
his old man's ears still growing as he shrinks.
Our hands in identical blue woollen gloves
link us like cut-out children.

He tries to get up. Can't.
I have to manoevre him onto all-fours,
put my arms round his waist and pull.

Funeral Plans

Somewhere upstairs
my father's planing down his coffin,
plump curls of pale oak
litter the floor.
He's been to B&Q for shiny screws,
top-of-the-range brass fittings.

Last week he was all eco-friendly,
made a boat for his ashes
out of tissue paper and bamboo.
Tested in the bath, it sank too fast
so he changed the angle of the sides,
used cow-gum instead of flour-and-water-paste.
You can float me off Jenny Brown's Point, he said.

Bang, bang, bang – today he's back with Plan A,
hammering with intent. I hope the wood
doesn't split. We haven't got another tree
to spare. This one scored a groove
all along the landing.
There's a hole in the garden
a cow could fall down.

We discuss the interior.
I tell him purple is for royalty
so he opts for orange,
my least favourite colour.
While we're at it, I say,
do you want to wear your suit
or will you be going casual?

My suit please, he says,
with a starched white handkerchief
in the breast pocket.
I wouldn't be seen dead in anything else.

Bedroom

When she couldn't manage the stairs,
she had to sleep in the dining-room
full of hard furniture
and no view.

How she missed her saggy old bed and its tunes,
her dressing-table's cloudy mirror,
her wardrobe's smell.

She begged us –
take me upstairs just once. Carry me.
I want to look out of the window.
I want to go through my drawers.

We couldn't, though I brought down her glove box,
ropes of beads which had a gritty feel,
a bag of buttons she traipsed her fingers through.

Now her heart beats close as a watch under a pillow
as I lie in her lumpy bed
on sheets mended down the middle,
watch the seven trees outside
through windows she would never curtain.

The Tear

Dad always called Mum his angel.
When she died I was six,
ran one night to his bed,
found Mum's side filled
by a huge wooden one.
It had massive wings
which lay stiff on the sheet
and carved yellow curls.
I hit it with my fist,
shouted in its ear.
Although it didn't blink,
I must have said something
because a wooden tear
wobbled on its eyelid,
rolled down its cheek like a bead
into the bedclothes.

Weather

It broke the day after she died,
rain plummeting from purple clouds,
the force of the wind breaking their fence.
A black bin-bag blew up into the pear tree,
stayed snagged for eight years;

eight years since she went to bed early
saying surely tonight it would thunder,
her head was aching, even the clock had clogged
in the sultry air.

He followed at his usual time, found her restless,
sheets bunched in her hands.
Are the windows closed? she said.
Is everything off? I'm worried about lightning.
Don't have a bath, it can spurt through the tap
and kill you.

Writing a Love Poem

During her absence,
I sit down to write.
Her fingertips dance on my pen;
her breath, apple-sweet,
mists the page,
her tongue as fragrant
as a coil of peel.

I rest my head on my words.
That's when I hear her
step through the night,
bend to the book,
put her thumb in the place.
Her hair spills over the paper,
down the binding.

Ten Places Where I See My Mother

Mondays, in the kitchen, her arms all suds.
I peer through steam but she's disappeared
till I see her in the yard, pegging sheets.
Later she'll be upstairs, taking off her wet blue dress
or coming out of the bathroom saying,
Don't use too much paper. We're quite low.

In the dark she's in different places:
the end of my bed, the space by the wardrobe,
picking up my clothes.
Fuzzy yellow light runs in ribbons
from her head to her heels.
Her footprints glow for ages after she's gone.

Today she's in the greenhouse
wearing gloves that are far too big
and the old straw hat.
I tap on the glass but she looks right through me.
I wish she'd smile, come close,
stroke back the fringe from my forehead.

Sundays, I see her under the earth,
peacefully asleep, her mouth slightly open,
but she comes to when I start arranging flowers.
Going home in the car, she sits beside me
folding the cellophane to use again,
winding the string round her little finger.

Speaking With the Dead

For this you should wear old pyjamas
with frayed hems and missing buttons.
The dead like to feel superior.
If you're having a bad-hair day,
they'll sit on your bed smiling,
toss sleek black curls,
smooth down robes with elegant fingers.

Put them in a good mood
if you want communication.
Don't let smell put you off,
how they talk without tongues,
how you can see right through them,
how they haven't any organs.

All they want is to hear how beautiful they are.
Play along.
Make no mention of their crimes
or they'll turn away without a backward glance
and the last you'll see will be boneless feet
with glass-bottomed soles
exiting through the ceiling.

Angels in the North

There's no call for them up here,
people say when asked,
we can do our own gardens,
but if you get up early
you can see them working secretly,
bent low over flowerbeds,
wings hooked up,
halos in their pockets.

They keep their faces averted
but the press of their feet
on dead grass revives it;
they bring roses back to life
just by touching them.
Their golden eyes can heal holes in petals,
make them colour up again,
get back their fleshiness and scent.

They repair the eyes of flowers we call weeds
which to angels are truly beautiful,
give back to trees their clack, clack,
their strong rustle.
Into orchards they stream their power,
leave their shape in the blossom's froth,
gifts of apples in the pantry.
And another thing you may not know:

vegetable gardens are their speciality.
They can sweeten the most stubborn carrots
so they flame orange in the ground.

Wallflowers

He's lost his wings,
they fell off somewhere by the side of the road
when he was admiring wallflowers.

I've brought you some, he says,
producing them crushed in his hanky,
still wet, smelling of his pocket.

I offer to go back and look
but he's happy to sit down and eat lunch.
This chair is wonderfully comfy, he admits,
without them.

Minding the Angels

They like the secret places by lakes or rivers
but someone still has to keep an eye on them,
make sure no one's taking photographs
or disturbing their peace.

They enjoy a bit of a paddle,
hang their wings on a tree.
One of them lights a fire.
He only has to point his halo at the twigs
and they catch.

The tallest gets the fish.
He wades right out,
his golden eyes transfigure the water.
Fish leap into his arms.
He pulls out the front of his robe
to carry them back.

There's a plump one who guts
then cooks; hums loudly while he's doing it.
The others tell him to hurry up,
they can get quite shirty when they're hungry.

The most beautiful one magics four stools
out of thin air. He's not supposed to do that.
They have remembered to bring bread.
It crumbles into their laps as they eat.
Grease trickles down their fingers.

They rinse them in the lake,
strip off for a swim.
They have perfect bodies but no sexual organs.
We can see their golden arms
breaking from the water,
their slicked back hair.

Then they fall asleep on the shingle,
bare feet dirty underneath like ours.